W9-BVA-875
ILLINOIS CENTRAL COLLEGE
PS3552.E75B7
C.2 STACKS
The broken ground.
A12900 393736
PS
3552
.E75
B7
c.2
BERRY
The broken ground
WITHDRAWN
Illinois Central College
Learning Resource Center

THE BROKEN GROUND

ALSO BY WENDELL BERRY

Nathan Coulter
A NOVEL

November Twenty-Six, Nineteen Hundred Sixty-Three
A POEM, WITH DRAWINGS BY BEN SHAHN

THE BROKEN GROUND

Poems by Wendell Berry, 1934-

Harcourt, Brace & World, Inc. *New York*

The author thanks the Guggenheim Foundation for
a year of working time, during which a number
of these poems were written.

Some of the poems in this volume previously appeared in *The Chelsea Review*, *Contact #3*, *Epoch*, *Heights Daily News*, *Limbo*, *The Nation*, *Poetry*, and *Prairie Schooner*.

first edition

Library of Congress Catalog Card Number: 64-18279

Printed in the United States of America

For my mother and father

CONTENTS

ELEGY

Pryor Thomas Berry
March 4, 1864–February 23, 1946

1

All day our eyes could find no resting place.
Over a flood of snow sight came back
Empty to the mind. The sun
In a shutter of clouds, light
Staggered down the fall of snow.
All circling surfaces of earth were white.
No shape or shadow moved the flight
Of winter birds. Snow held the earth its silence.
We could pick no birdsong from the wind.
At nightfall our father turned his eyes away.
It was this storm of silence shook out his ghost.

2

We sleep; he only wakes
Who is unshapen in a night of snow.
His shadow in the shadow of the earth
Moves the dark to wholeness.
We watch beside his body here, his image
Shape of silence in the room.

3

Sifting
Down the wind, the winter rain
Spirals about the town
And the church hill's jut of stones.
Under the mounds, below
The weather's moving, the numb dead know
No fitfulness of wind.

On the road that in his knowledge ends
We bear our father to the earth.
We have adorned the shuck of him
With flowers as for a bridal, burned
Lamps about him, held death apart
Until the grave should mound it whole.

Behind us rain breaks the corners
Of our father's house, quickens
On the downslope to noise.
                                        Our steps
Clamor in his silence, who tracked
The sun to autumn in the dust.
                                              Below the hill
The river bears the rain away, that cut
His fields their shape and stood them dry.

Water wearing the earth
Is the shape of the earth,
The river flattening in its bends.
Their mingling held
Ponderable in his words—
Knowledge polished on a stone.

4
River and earth and sun and wind disjoint,
Over his silence flow apart. His words
Are sharp to memory as cold rain
But are not ours.
                              We stare dumb
Upon the fulcrum dust, across which death
Lifts up our love. There is no more to add
To this perfection. We turn away
Into the shadow of his death.

Time in blossom and fruit and seed,
Time in the dust huddles in his darkness.
The world, spun in its shadow, holds all.
Until the morning comes his death is ours.

Until morning comes say of the blind bird:
His feet are netted with darkness, or he flies
His heart's distance into the darkness of his eyes.
A season's sun will light him no tree green.

5

Spring tangles shadow and light,
Branches of trees
Knit vision and wind.
The shape of the wind is a tree
Bending, spilling its birds.
From the cloud to the stone
The rain stands tall,
Columned into his darkness.
Water over blanched bones
Jangles in a forest of roots.
The church hill heals our father in.
Our remembering moves from a different place.

DIAGON

for Tanya

1

In the riven channel torqued in its bends
Movements of fish, swaying of sunken trees
Fledge no light. Days ride adrift
At the mirror surface.
                                        By night the great fish
Hunt the shallows, their silent breathing
Opening red flowers of their gills. At dawn
They sound from their feeding.
                                                  The current
In its troughed motion moves the foundered dark
Where the drowned men set their souls afloat.
In their clotted eyes the dark is whole,
Their vision unlidded by no shadow's shape.
They dive more lightly than fish
In the twisted eddies.
                                        I recall the men
Of no hope who built them boats of stone,
The shape of my face afloat,
A black leaf washed over the eyes.

I have felt the water flow
In the hollow where my hand folds.

2

Since morning rain fell
Down the valley, the river
Booming at the top of its banks,
Blackbirds raucous on driftlogs,
Riding the branches of wrecked trees.

In their stilted houses
The river men sleep
Fitful in their sweated beds.

In their dreams fish
Enter the squared windows,
Brown water curls
Over the thresholds.

Rain steady past darkfall,
I lean to the thickening water
Raising the lines, the boat's bow
Nudged to the channel's black,
The sun cooled and dark
In the river's stones.

My blunted eyes fail
At my hands' shape,
Black water holds no image
Of my face. I have become
My shadow leaned above water.
In my mind's dark I hang
With the hooks in my hands,
Swing in the fishtail currents.

To the high-porched house,
The white room composed by the waiting lamp,
I return from the hooked night.
But this fastening remains;
I am derived from my death,
Marked by the black river.
With this knowledge I will enter morning.

3
After the floods of spring
The river men return
To their hollow doorways
In the broken valley,
Cross the chaos of mud
Where no foot track
Cups its shadow.

In the days of rain
The valley leveled
With the brown flood.
The massed water held
The hill trough beyond beginning
In the darkness of fish.
In the crippled eyes
Of the river men
No known shape twisted
A word from their tongues.

The fingers of the river
Slide from the doorposts,
Its water quieted
In the maimed channel.

In silence the river men
Watch morning shape itself
On the drying valley,
Whose mud shape assumes
The solidity of shadow,
In the river men's eyes
Transfixed as stone.

The river's injury is its shape.

4

At the first bird's cry night breaks.
The sun moves from its past light
Into this morning, forces the dark
To tree shapes around my house.
My wakened shadow unjoins from sleep.

The sun sets vision afloat,
Its hard glare down
All the reaches of the river,
Light on the wind waves
Running to shore. Under the light
River and hill divide. Two dead
White trees stand in the water,

The shimmering river casts
A net of light around them,
Their snagged shapes break through.

At noon the wind lays.
The trees stand on the banks
With their shadows beside them
Undisturbed, the leaves quiet
In their spear shapes. The sky
Lies flat on the water, blue
On green, their colors together.
In green water two white clouds
Move deeply.

The horizons of this valley,
The folded hills
Have the breadth of an eyelid.
Entering my eyes, the sky
Is no larger than a coin.
The point of the sun
In my eyes
Will become a darkness.

5
A broad flower
Lying on its green curving stem
Is this valley

It is a flower of durable blooming
Complete in no season
But in its moments full-formed
As a bird flying

Colors of the hills
Its petals fall
And are renewed

In spring the whites
Of dogwood and plum
Brown of plowed ground

In summer a weaving of greens
Of willow and sycamore
Broad fields green with corn

In autumn red
Of sumac and oak
Thickets lighted with goldenrod

Winter brings no closing
White trunks
Of the sycamores
Stand in the snow

The days of this summer
Are many-colored on the hills
Red with the slant light
Of evenings and mornings

Green in the dry light of noon
Entering blue of distance
Where the sky bends on them

They lean toward the sun

At night the flower is black
Or night is another flower
Blooming on day shape

Past the sleep of lovers
In the darkened houses
Its blooming changes

Its shape is the shape
Of all rains

THE RIVER VOYAGERS

1

Where the light's bells ring
Morning on the river,
Waking the town to its round of spires
And burials, is only half
The world. This very light shapes a country
Green of leaf and river
Within the sleep of the dead voyagers,
Or their death also
Is a river where morning returns
And is welcome.
The scarlet bird chanting
Its renewal in a tree of shade
As constantly sings
To their earthen unhearing ears.

2

The ghosts of the voyagers are gay
In the total sleep of their bones.
From the green noon shade of the river
Their vision slowly loves the sky,
Accepting bird flight, dawn and dark.
Rage for flesh and possession over,
They are gentle now. Their boats, swamped
With voyages and drowned, release the stream.
Through the broad country of their sleep,
Burnished towers and belfries of the sun,
The river runs to noon forever.
The clear light rings with bees.

OBSERVANCE

The god of the river leans
against the shore in the early
morning, resting from his caprices;

the gentle sun parades
on his runneled gaze—he devotes
himself to watching it as one
devotes oneself to sleep;
                                        the light becomes
his consciousness, warming him.

The river clears after the winter
floods; the slopes of the hills renew
the sun, diaphanous flower and leaf, blue-green
with distance, patina of their substantial
bronze which continues them from spring
to spring;
                the idle god dallies
in his shade, his mind adorned with stones.

At the river's edge there is singing;
the townsmen have come down from their sleep,
their singing silences the birds;
they sing renewal beyond irreparable
divisions.
                The god did not expect
these worshippers, but he hears
them singing, briefly as reeds
grown up by the water;
                                        they go
away, the river re-enters
their silence
                    —and he watches
a white towboat approach, shoving
its rust-colored island of barges,

the sound of its engines filling his mind
and draining out;
                                        the forked wake
wrinkles on his vision, pointing
to the corner of his eye,
and floats away;
                                    the holiday fishermen
arrive—
                    a man and his wife
establish themselves on a sandbar, bringing
lunch in a basket, blankets, tackle
down the path through the young
horseweeds;
                            the woman smooths
a blanket on the sand, and begins
a ponderous sunbath, her eyes
covered, her skirt hoisted
above her knees;
                                    the man
casts a baited line downstream
and uncaps a beer:
                                        the god observes;
these are the sundry
objects of his thought.

He has watched the passing
of other boats, assemblages,
seasons, inundations,
                                            boatmen
whose voyages bore down the currents
to the dark shores of their eyes

—and has forgotten them, innocent
of his seasonal wraths, his mischiefs
accomplished and portending, as his present
forbearance is innocent;

the direction
of the river, persisting under floods,
continues, counterpoint and form
to his disjointed moods;

the perfection
of his forgetting allows the sun
to glitter

—the light
flows away, its blue and white
peeling off the green waves.

His thought does not advance
from memory, nor anticipate
from any desire;

his mind contains
the river as its banks
contain it, in a single act
receiving it and letting it go;
his eyes divide its mottled movement
dispassionately as shadows.

BOONE

Beyond this final house
I'll make no journeys, that is
the nature of this place,
I came here old; the house contains
the shade of its walls,
a fire in winter; I know
from what direction to expect the wind;
still
        I move in the descent
of days from what was dreamed
to what remains.
In the stillness of this single place
where I'm resigned to die
I'm not free of journeys:
one eye watches while the other sleeps
—every day is a day's remove
from what I knew.

We held a country in our minds
which, unpossessed, allowed
the encroachment of our dreams;
our vision descended like doves
at morning on valleys still blue
in the extremity of hills
until we moved in a prodigy of reckonings,
sustaining in the toil of a journey
the rarity of our desire.

We came there at the end of spring,
climbing out of the hill's shadow
in the evening,
                    the light
leaned quiet on the trees,
we'd foreseen no words;
after nightfall when the coals of our fire
contained all that was left
of vision, my journey relinquished me
to sleep;
            kindling in the uneasy
darkness where we
broached our coming to the place we'd dreamed
the dying green of those valleys
began to live.

My passage grew into that country
like a vine, as if remaining
when I'd gone, responsive to the season's
change, boding a continuance of eyes;
not the place or the distance
made it known to me,
but the direction so ardently obeyed,
preserving my advance
on the edge of virgin light,
broken by my shadow's stride;
I wouldn't recognize the way back.

I approach my death, descend
toward the last fact; it is
not so clear to me now as it once seemed;
when I hunted in the new lands
alone, I could foresee
the skeleton hiding with its wound
after the fear and flesh were gone;
                                        now
it may come as a part of sleep.

In winter the river hides its flowing under the ice
—even then it flows,
bearing interminably down; the black crow flies
into the black night;
the bones of the old dead ache for the house fires.

Death is a conjecture of the seed
and the seasons bear it out;
the wild plum achieves its bloom,
perfects the yellow center of each flower,
submits to violence—
extravagance too grievous for praise;
there are no culminations, no
requitals.

Freed of distances
and dreams, about to die,
the mind turns back to its approaches:
what else have I known?

The search
withholds the joy from what is found,
that has been my sorrow;
love is no more than what remains
of itself.

There are no arrivals.

At the coming of winter
the birds obey the leviathan flock
that moves them south,
a rhythm of the blood that survives the cold
in pursuit of summer;
and the sun, innocent of time
as the blossom is innocent of ripeness,
faithful to solstice, returns—
and the flocks return;
the season recognizes them.

If it were possible now
I'd make myself submissive
to the weather
as an old tree, without retrospect
of winter, blossoming,
grateful for summers hatched from thrushes' eggs
in the speckled thickets
—obedient
to darkness,
be innocent of my dying.

GREEN AND WHITE

The wind scruffing it, the bay
is like a field of green grass,

and the white seagulls afloat
in the hackling of the green bay
are like white flowers blooming
in the field,

                                        for they are white
and come there, and are still
a while, and leave, and leaving
leave no sign they ever were there.

Green is no memorial to white.

There's danger in it. They fly
beyond idea till they come back.

BE STILL IN HASTE

How quietly I
begin again

from this moment
looking at the
clock, I start over

so much time has
passed, and is equaled
by whatever
split-second is present

from this
moment this moment
is the first

NINE VERSES OF THE SAME SONG

1

the ear finely attuned
to the extravagant music
of yellow pears ripening
in the scrolled light
of orchards as if the world
were perfect
hears the cicada burst its shell

2

the quiet man sits
touching his cheek
in a room delicately walled
with the sound of rain

trumpets on the phonograph
hold the globed gold light
belling in the mirror's corridor
time out of time
a dance of instant light
in the mirror's silent hallway

counter-measure
to clock-tick
the morning-red cockerel's
burnished crowing
heard mute in the sun-tattered
darkness of gravestones
and loud
in the quick of his wrist

3

state fair

the perfect green
and red and yellow gold
of this prized and pampered fruit
sheaves of millet
sheaves of wheat
arranged in perfect ripeness
beyond our touch
to music out the light

as if all possibilities of seed
became visible and orderly here
and ripeness final

but as the sign cautions
do not touch

perfection is the myth of effort

from here we endlessly return

4

hear also the resounding actual
music of wood and bow

played alone
sounds of the flesh without soul

like the austere strained-for
music of pure soul

music of the unplayed strings
imaged in the mind's ear

it is a more mingled music
we are fated to

a speech breaking categories
to confront its objects

rapt cicadas thrumming
the ear's meat

beyond this light
and darkness are the same

5
in starlight
slow as a ship
the whitened carcass founders
and goes down
earth like water
caving the ribs

bees in the hollow skull
make honey
as gold in the dark
as light

6

the picnic done with
we became aware
of the black bull at his mating

imaged in us the music
more gay than madrigals
that strummed his veins
parading
to his perfect lust

deep-bodied
slow
he stood a moment attentive
to the drumming of his blood

then mounted
brought the period
to its close

and descended
to the immediacy of darkness
and grass
unwintered and green
to his quieted flesh
as if only the hour
awaited him

to our ears the evening cicadas
whirred like violins
their dry atmospheric sound

7

two definitive movements

my child stood in the doorway
watching night approach the house
asking to be allowed outside

and admission granted to the dark
she chose the light instead

that

and the word *gone*
she learned to say
at the summer's end

she has touched knowing's edge
and will own it
closely as her flesh

the morning-glory's opening
the white tenuous muscle
flexing to light
as though no darkness had ever been
is not profounder music

8

and my love has come to me
to ask my comfort
for the hurt I give her
—having no other

time and again

for that trammel me
my heart

my hearing suffers
no more sorrowing music

9

the child born dead
goes free of light

bears all time with him
rounded to his grave

in this my dusty-faced
fathers let go the world

grass stems wind back
into the seed

the stones perfectly
contain their stillness

his muteness holds
a consummate prayer

A MAN WALKING AND SINGING

for James Baker Hall

1

It is no longer necessary to sleep
in order to dream of our destruction.

We take form within our death, the figures
emerging like shadows in fire.

Who is it? speaking to me of death's beauty.

I think it is my own black angel, as near me
as my flesh. I am never divided from his darkness.
His face is the black mask of my face. My eyes
live in his black eye-holes. On his black wings
I rise to sing.
                    His mouthing presences attend
my singing, masquerading his black ambiguous
absolute:
               Die more lightly than live,
they say. Death is more gay.
                              There's no argument
against its certainty, at least, they say.

I know they know as surely as I live my death
exists, and has my shape.

2

But the man so forcefully walking,
say where he goes,
say what he hears and what he sees
and what he knows
to cause him to stride so merrily.

He goes in spring
through the evening street
to buy bread,

green trees leaning
over the sidewalk,
forsythia yellow
beneath the windows,
birds singing
as birds sing
only in spring,

and he sings, his footsteps
beating the measure of his song.

In an open window
a man and a woman
leaning together
at the room's center
embrace and kiss
as if they met
in passing,
the spring wind
lifting the curtain.

His footsteps carry him
past the window,
deeper into his song.

His singing becomes conglomerate
of all he sees,
leaving the street behind him
runged as a ladder
or the staff of a song.

3

To his death? Yes.

He walks and sings to his death.

And winter will equal spring.

And for the lovers, even
while they kiss, even though
it is spring, the day ends.

But to the sound of his passing
he sings. It is a kind of triumph
that he grieves—thinking
of the white lilacs in bloom,
profuse, fragrant, white
in excess of all seasonal need,

and of the mockingbird's crooked
arrogant notes, hooking him to the sky
as though no flight
or dying could equal him
at his momentary song.

THE APPLE TREE

for Ann and Dick O'Hanlon

In the essential prose
of things, the apple tree
stands up, emphatic
among the accidents
of the afternoon, solvent,
not to be denied.
The grass has been cut
down, carefully
to leave the orange
poppies still in bloom;
the tree stands up
in the odor of the grass
drying. The forked
trunk and branches are
also a kind of necessary
prose—shingled with leaves,
pigment and song
imposed on the blunt
lineaments of fact, a foliage
of small birds among them.
The tree lifts itself up
in the garden, the
clutter of its green
leaves halving the light,
stating the unalterable
congruity and form
of its casual growth;
the crimson finches appear
and disappear, singing
among the design.

THE COMPANIONS

When he goes out in the morning
and comes back at night
his landlady is there

watching him, leaning
forward in her chair, one hand
holding the curtain back,

simply curious, simply old,
having stashed away her knickknacks
in three commemorative rooms,

stored up a winter's breathing,
forbidden the cold
to come in. She dreams

she's dying in her sleep
and wakes up afraid, to breathe in
again her breathed-out breath.

Who will outlast?
She waits for him, faithful
to his arrivals and to the place;

he brings back life to her,
what he salvages of himself daily
from the shut-out air.

They don't speak.
She just observes his homecoming,
lifelike in her chair

as the shell of a wan moth
holding to the lace.

THE ARISTOCRACY

Paradise might have appeared here,
surprising us, a tackle of sublime coordinates
figuring over the trees, surprising us, even
though the look of the place seems not
altogether unexpectant of such an advent,
seems not altogether willing to settle
for something less: the fine light
prepared in the taut statuary of the oaks;
venerable churches of muted brick;
Greek porches presiding at the ends
of approaches; delicate fanlights over doorways
delicate and symmetrical as air, if air
prepared, preened itself for Paradise
to appear, surprisingly, but not very, in the place
—all it needs to *be* Paradise is populace.

(What has appeared, surprisingly, but not very
—stepping out the door, and down the steps,
groping for each next-lower step
with a left foot her expansive exquisitely garmented
paunch has prevented her seeing for thirty-five
years—is a rich, fat, selfish,
spavined, ugly, ignorant, old
bitch, airing her cat.)

THE BIRD KILLER

His enemy, the universe, surrounds him nightly with stars
going nowhere over the cold woods that has grown now,
with nightfall, totally dark, the stars deeper in the sky
than darkness; his thoughts go out alone into the winds
of the woods' dark. He sits in the doorway and softly
plays the guitar; his fingers are stiff and heavy
and touch the strings, not dextrously, so that he plays
his own song, no true copy of a tune; sometimes the notes
go away from melody, form singly, and die out,
singly, in the hollow of the instrument, like single small
lights in the dark; his music has this passion,
that he plays as he can play. All day he has walked
in the woods with his gun, ruin of summer, iron-rust,
crumpled bronze, under the bare trees, devouring song. Now
the trees of darkness grow tall and wide; nobody's
silence is in the woods. In the hush of all birds
who love light, he lets go free to die in the broad woods
in the dark the notes of his song.

THE COUNTRY TOWN IN EARLY SUMMER MORNING

The town has grown here, angular
and white on its hill pelted
with thickets, in the passage
of a darkness, in the black
filled hollows of its time, its
history of acts and briars.
It rose up with the first
singing and light to surprise
its dreamers. Among the slopes
and groves of the inert hill,
channeled and splined by the
seasonal escapade of streams,
where its graves and garbage
choke the ravines, old shoes
in a milling of stones commemorate
the town laid waste. By morning's
instantaneous contrivance, mottled
shade and light, the day upholds
carved orange lilies in a calm
dreamers no longer dream but know.

AN ARCHITECTURE

Like a room, the clear stanza
of birdsong opens among the noises
of motors and breakfasts.

Among the light's beginnings,
lifting broken grey of the night's
end, the bird hastens to his song

as to a place, a room commenced
at the end of sleep. Around
him his singing is entire.

A FIT OF WINTER

The body, exhumed from sleep,
is strange to its waking
—a perch for the eyes.

Bells stroke the syllables
of another language.
In the night it rained.

After the shedding of petals
there's left the abstract
dry fist of seed.

What it may have meant
held out against the asking.

CANTICLE
for Robert Hazel

1
What death means is not this—
the spirit, triumphant in the body's fall,
praising its absence, feeding on music.
If life can't justify and explain itself,
death can't justify and explain it.
A creed and a grave never did equal the life
of anything. Yellow flowers sprout in the clefts
of ancient stones at the beginning of April.
The black clothes of the priests are turned
against the frail yellow of sunlight and petal;
they wait in their blackness to earn joy
by dying. They trust that nothing holy is free,
and so their lives are paid. Money slots
in the altar rails can make a jukebox of the world,
the mind paying its gnawed coins for the safety of ignorance.

2
Now while blood and heat run in the mind,
yellow flowers gouging out of the cracked stones
bloom into a consuming question
which is its own answer, and is all.
There's nothing here but earth, no matter what it buries.

3

The black face of the coal merchant opens with his singing,
and his blackened lungs breathe out his song.
He mentions the daily and several colors of the world.
His song is part of a singing into which the trees
move, and fill themselves with all their living
and their sounds. Dirt and offal assail the dead
with music, and they vanish out of their bodies.
The coal man laughs in the black of his opened doorway;
in his sooty face his mouth filled with laughter
is like a red tulip blooming out of the dirt;
his eyes are clarified, seeing the young leaves
over his doorway drop their shadows at his feet;
his laughter is useful as money and holy as altars.
Now the hyacinths are full born. The rain is on them.
They are like nothing ever imagined or written down.
I choose and sing these shapes and breathings of the ground.
I wear this yellow blossom like an eye.

THE MORNING BLUE

Over the roofs and long shadows
and new-leafed trees, the
shingling of voices and engines:
a perfected ocean patiently
opening and shining. Birds,
gables, journeys, clouds, trees
take their odd sure places in it.
Here is what the night has turned to.

SPARROW

A sparrow is
his hunger organized.
Filled, he flies
before he knows he's going to.
And he dies by the
same movement: filled
with himself, he goes
by the eye-quick
reflex of his flesh
out of sight,
leaving his perfect
absence without a thought.

AN OLD WOMAN FEEDING THE BIRDS

The old woman stands by the lake in the park,
the snag of an old tree friendly to birds,
nearly hidden by the black she mourns in
for the loss of all but herself.
I wonder what satisfaction it can give her
to feed these wild things that belong to nobody.
And then I know that for her, in her enclosing
blackness, having lived so long,
to see the completely living eat is real.

A MUSIC

I employ the blind mandolin player
in the tunnel of the Métro. I pay him
a coin as hard as his notes,
and maybe he has employed me, and pays me
with his playing to hear him play.

Maybe we're necessary to each other,
and this vacant place has need of us both
—it's vacant, I mean, of dwellers,
is populated by passages and absences.

By some fate or knack he has chosen
to place his music in this cavity
where there's nothing to look at
and blindness costs him nothing.
Nothing was here before he came.

His music goes out among the sounds
of footsteps passing. The tunnel is the resonance
and meaning of what he plays.
It's his music, not the place, I go by.

In this light which is just a fact, like darkness
or the edge or end of what you may be
going toward, he turns his cap up on his knees
and leaves it there to ask and wait, and holds up
his mandolin, the lantern of his world;

his fingers make their pattern on the wires.
This is not the pursuing rhythm
of a blind cane pecking in the sun,
but is a singing in a dark place.

TO GO BY SINGING

He comes along the street, singing,
a rag of a man, with his game foot and bum's clothes.
He's asking for nothing—his hands
aren't even held out. But he sings
by profession, nevertheless. His song
is the gift of singing, to him
and to all who will listen.

To hear him, you'd think the engines
would all stop, and the flower vendor would stand
with her hands full of flowers and not move.
You'd think somebody would have hired him
and provided him a clean quiet stage to sing on.

But there's no special occasion or place
for his singing—that's why it needs
to be strong. His song doesn't impede the morning
or change it, except by freely adding itself.

THE WILD

In the empty lot—a place
not natural, but wild—among
the trash of human absence,

the slough and shamble
of the city's seasons, a few
old locusts bloom.

A few woods birds
fly and sing
in the new foliage

—warblers and tanagers, birds
wild as leaves; in a million
each one would be rare,

new to the eyes. A man
couldn't make a habit
of such color,

such flight and singing.
But they're the habit of this
wasted place. In them

the ground is wise. They are
its remembrance of what it is.

MAY SONG

For whatever is let go
there's a taker.
The living discovers itself

where no preparation
was made for it,
where its only privilege

is to live if it can.
The window flies from the dark
of the subway mouth

into the sunlight
stained with the green
of the spring weeds

that crowd the improbable
black earth
of the embankment,

their stout leaves
like the tongues and bodies
of a herd, feeding

on the new heat,
drinking at the seepage
of the stones:

the freehold of life,
triumphant
even in the waste

of those who possess it.
But it is itself the possessor,
we know at last,

seeing it send out weeds
to take back
whatever is left:

Proprietor, pasturing foliage
on the rubble,
making use

of the useless—a beauty
we have less than not
deserved.

THE FEAR OF DARKNESS

The tall marigolds darken.
The baby cries
for better reasons than it knows.
The young wife walks
and walks among the shadows
meshed in the rooms.
And he sits in the doorway,
looking toward the woods,
long after the stars come out.
He feels the slow
sky turn toward him, and wait.
His birthright
is a third-hand Chevrolet,
bought for too much. "I
floorboard the son of a bitch,
and let her go."

THE PLAN

My old friend, the owner
of a new boat, stops by
to ask me to fish with him,

and I say I will—both of us
knowing that we may never
get around to it, it may be

years before we're both
idle again on the same day.
But we make a plan, anyhow,

in honor of friendship
and the fine spring weather
and the new boat

and our sudden thought
of the water shining
under the morning fog.

ON THE FRONT PORCH

"Did you know
your eyes can live
after you're dead?"

"No mam.
That's
your soul, I thought."

"Ha ha. Well,
it says here your eyes
can be removed

immediately after death
and transplanted
into another person."

"Wouldn't that be
horrible!
My

conscience!—to
see through a
dead man's eyes!"

ASCENT

1

This mud, my genesis,
slicks and shines
in the rinsed morning.

Under all my sleeps
the river has plodded its furrow
to be wakened to

—intact for all my days
have taken from it, the sum
of its running.

The meshes of the sun
leap up, netting the leaves
like schools of fish.

2

Walking on the world
in which the final explosion
is planted, arrived

at another waking, the body
recognizes itself gladly.
The familiar persists,

nothing but the night has gone.
Having made peace again
with the loss of time,

I climb the bent road
in the opening of the ledged stone,
in the crease of my mind,

a surface tension of the known
answering the weight
of my feet, bearing me

like a water-strider walking
on the roof of drowning.

3
The wind crossing it, the green field
moves in itself, into itself,
like the iris of my green eye.

Along the deep alleys of the grass
the living waken and go
in their commonwealth

toward whatever singing
the morning will carry
on its branches.

Under its shingles and leaves,
flight of bomber and hummingbird,
the town survives its nightmares

—colony of white mushrooms
grown up during the night
out of the leaf-fall of its grove.

THE GUEST

Washed into the doorway
by the wake of the traffic,
he wears humanity
like a third-hand shirt
—blackened with enough
of Manhattan's dirt to sprout
a tree, or poison one.
His empty hand has led him
where he has come to.
Our differences claim us.
He holds out his hand,
in need of all that's mine.

And so we're joined, as deep
as son and father. His life
is offered me to choose.

Shall I begin servitude
to him? Let this cup pass.
Who am I? But charity must
suppose, knowing no better,
that this is a man fallen
among thieves, or come
to this strait by no fault
—that our difference
is not a judgment,
though I can afford to eat
and am made his judge.

I am, I nearly believe,
the Samaritan who fell
into the ambush of his heart
on the way to another place.
My stranger waits, his hand
held out like something to read,
as though its emptiness
is an accomplishment.
I give him a smoke and the price
of a meal, no more

—not sufficient kindness
or believable sham.
I paid him to remain strange
to my threshold and table,
to permit me to forget him—
knowing I won't. He's the guest
of my knowing, though not asked.

THE THIEF

I think of us lying asleep,
eyes and hands filled with the dark,
when the arm of the night
entered, reaching into the pockets
of our empty clothes. We slept
in the element of that power,
innocent of it, preserved from it
not even by our wish.
As though not born, we were carried
beyond an imminence we did not
waken to, as passively as stars
are carried beyond their spent
shining—our eyes granted to the light
again, by what chance or price
we do not even know.

THE BROKEN GROUND

The opening out and out,
body yielding body:
the breaking
through which the new
comes, perching
above its shadow
on the piling up
darkened broken old
husks of itself:
bud opening to flower
opening to fruit opening
to the sweet marrow
of the seed—

                              taken
from what was, from
what could have been.
What is left
is what is.